A LIGHT IN THE DARKNESS

A LIGHT IN THE DARKNESS

Finding Solace Within Yourself

SKYE SAARELA

Is It Wet Yet Press

To those who are facing mental illness. You are not alone. There is a light that calls to you from the darkness; run towards it.

Copyright © 2022 by Skye Saarela

All rights reserved. No part of this book may be reproduced in any manner whatsoever without written permission except in the case of brief quotations embodied in critical articles and reviews.

First Printing, 2022

The Darkness

Chapter One:
The Darkness

I

What is Death?

Do you ever wonder about death?
Where do we go?
Who will we see?
I always wonder about death,
Where will I go?
Who will I see?
What is definition of death?
Is it an escape?
Is it a looping cycle?

II

See You Later

You're not a knight in shining armor,
you're not an angel sent from up above.
You're just a joke, a huge embarrassment,
you're the reason I do not want to find love.
You're so rude, you only care for yourself,
you're all an act, and I can see right through.
You're no saint; you are simply a sinner,
you're so spoiled, and you know it too.
You're not willing to change,
you're not one to admit you're wrong.
You're always pointing fingers, insecure,
you're killing me, and it's time I move along.

III

Chariot of Tears

I admit I do cry,
I cry a lot, and it's a fact.
I don't have to lie,
I don't have to put on an act.
I admit I'm fragile,
I break and shatter.
I am in a battle,
I can't escape this disaster.
I admit I do try,
I try my best to heal.
I just want to fly,
but my wings I cannot feel.
I admit I have pain,
I can't hide my fears.
I ride in the rain
with my chariot of tears.

IV

Downed Power Line

There was an explosion of colors,
they emitted from you and me.
There was more to discover,
however, the explosions ceased.
Undeniable electricity,
a shock when we locked eyes.
Short-circuited, there was toxicity,
and we couldn't fix it this time.

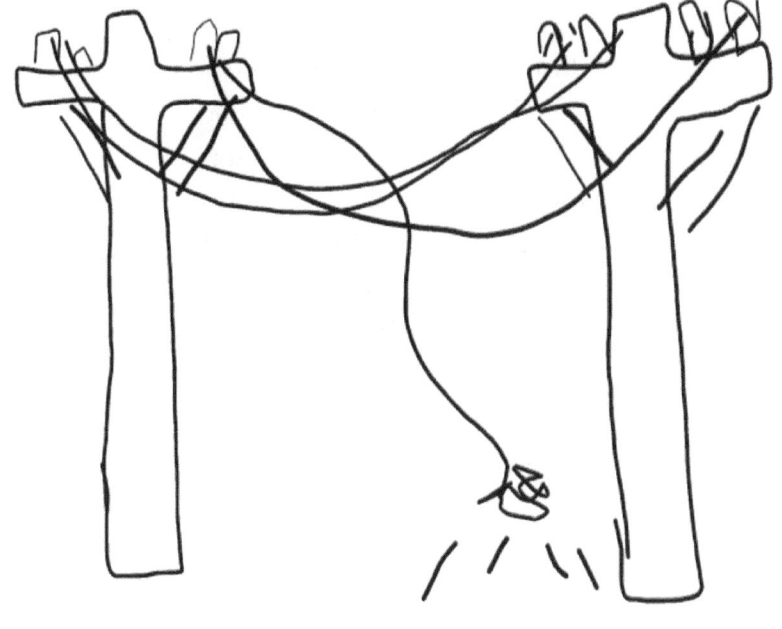

V

How Dare You

How dare you question my loyalty,
and how dare you act like you're a friend.
How dare you talk behind my back,
and my trust in you is ending.
How dare you ask if he's happy,
and how dare you try to change his mind.
How dare you even bring that up?
My view of you is no longer kind.
How dare you blatantly hurt me,
and how dare you think that this is okay?
How dare you think this is fine,
and my love for you has gone away.

VI

Echoes

I hear the echoes of your voice,
and it still haunts me to this day.
I wish that I had the choice,
the choice to make it go away.
I have visions of your pain,
it wakes me up at night.
I have nothing to gain,
I endure an endless fight.
I want to erase it all,
but it never seems to end.
I try to fly but always fall,
a wound I cannot mend.
I tried to make peace,
accept that you're gone.
The nightmares never cease,
I'm surprised I survived till dawn.

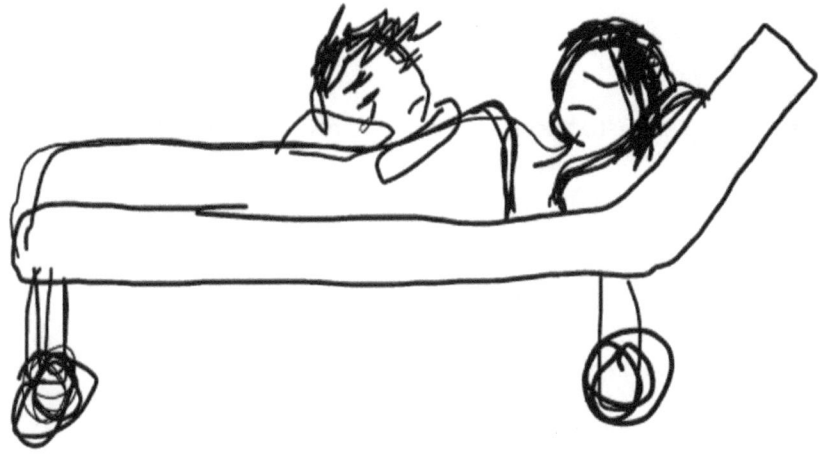

VII

Staying Sober

Can you just stop?
Can you please just leave me alone?
Stop tempting me,
stop trying to corrupt my sober mind.
I cover my eyes,
I cover my eyes, hoping you will go.
Leave my home,
leave me and all our memories behind.

VIII

Nightmare

Heaven has thrown you out,
and you have fallen from grace.
Your sins were too loud,
and your home is now this place.
The golden gates stay sealed,
and you aren't allowed back in.
Your horns revealed,
and now let the torment begin.
You're drowning in your despair,
and there isn't anyone to help you.
You're not an angel,
and you've broken your halo.
You'll remain underground,
no one to save you now,
you can't escape from here,
so welcome to your nightmare.

IX

Ill Wishes

I curse your name,
I wish nothing but pain,
you are the one to blame,
and you are so insane.
You destroyed my heart.
You've caused so much damage.
I want to rip you apart,
and I would be so savage.
I don't believe it,
they buy into your lies,
your stories are a hit,
and the truth I hope they'll find.
I am sick of you,
I wish you'd drop dead,
I want you to lose,
and I don't take back what I've said.

X

Self-doubt

I have been a mess lately,
I am a wreck most days,
I am a crime, you see,
I am a light that fades.
I am a shattered soul,
I am a failure, you know,
I am a worthless goal,
I am so easy to throw.
I hate my mind,
I am trapped deep within.
I am falling behind,
I am letting my demons win.

XI

Playing the Victim

I wake up with good intentions,
I only want good vibes.
It all goes downhill when you appear,
my good vibes vanish.
Complaining about how your life sucks,
do you ever have fun?
Maybe, just maybe, you need to change,
you need to rearrange.
I grow tired of the passive aggression,
you're not one for discussion.
You can't escape your hot mess ways,
there's no helping you, so go away.

XII

Wrecking Me

I've given you all I could,
you cannot see the truth,
deep down, I know you should,
but I can't handle this abuse.
I've given you all of me,
you cannot see my heart,
deep down, you should believe,
you destroyed us from the start.
You tear me down,
you break me into pieces,
I'm lying on the ground,
broken for no reason.
You just keep on twisting me,
breaking me,
you just keep on bending me,
wrecking me.

XIII

Casket

Words that cut like a blade,
true love that starts to fade.
My soul is breaking now,
and my heart is darker now.
This damage will not heal,
I forgot how to feel.
My flame is colder now,
my light is fading out.
I'm losing my mind,
I am beyond repair.
My faith I cannot find,
trapped in despair.
So nail my casket shut,
be sure it's secure.
I'm a plague, and I disgust,
I know there's no cure.

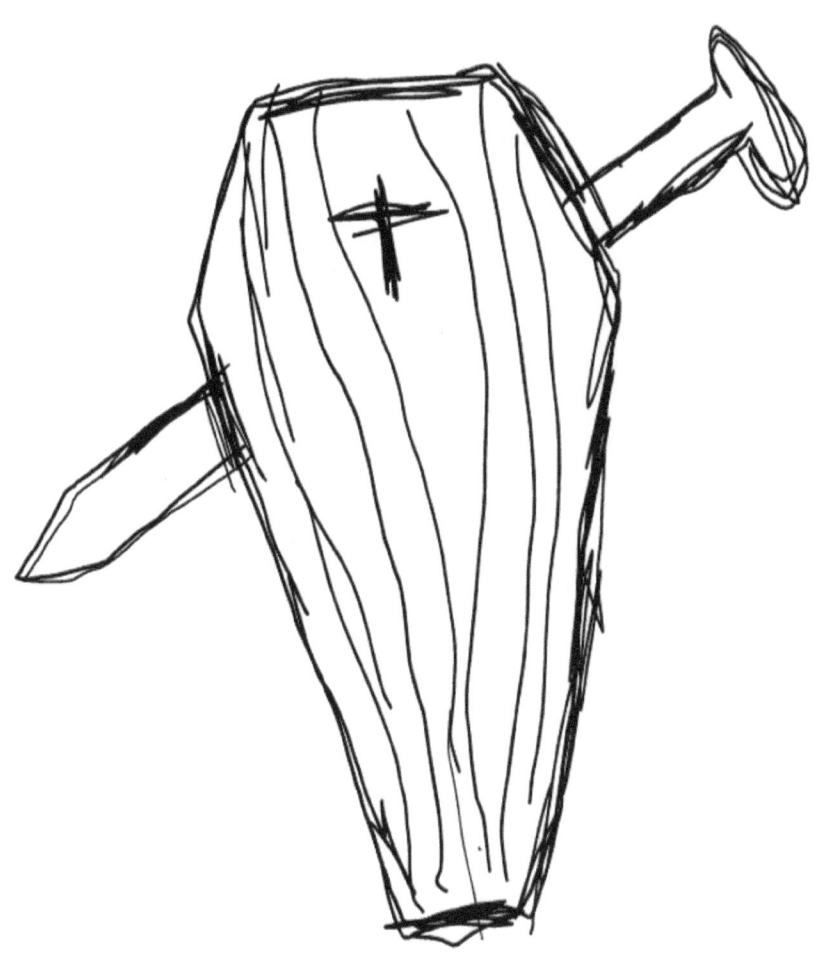

XIV

Being Alone

They wonder if I'm okay,
they want me to hangout,
I tell them *not today*,
they just cry and pout.
I don't want company,
I don't want to fake laugh,
being alone, I'd rather be,
rip their invitations in half.

XV

Sinking

Rainy days are more common now,
at least inside my head.
Rainy days turn into major floods,
and it fills my lungs with dread.
The water current takes me with it,
and I try to swim to shore.
The water current becomes more violent,
and it's so much stronger than before.
Underneath the water, I'm screaming,
and nobody can hear my voice.
Underneath the water, I'm sinking,
and there is no other choice.

The Voice

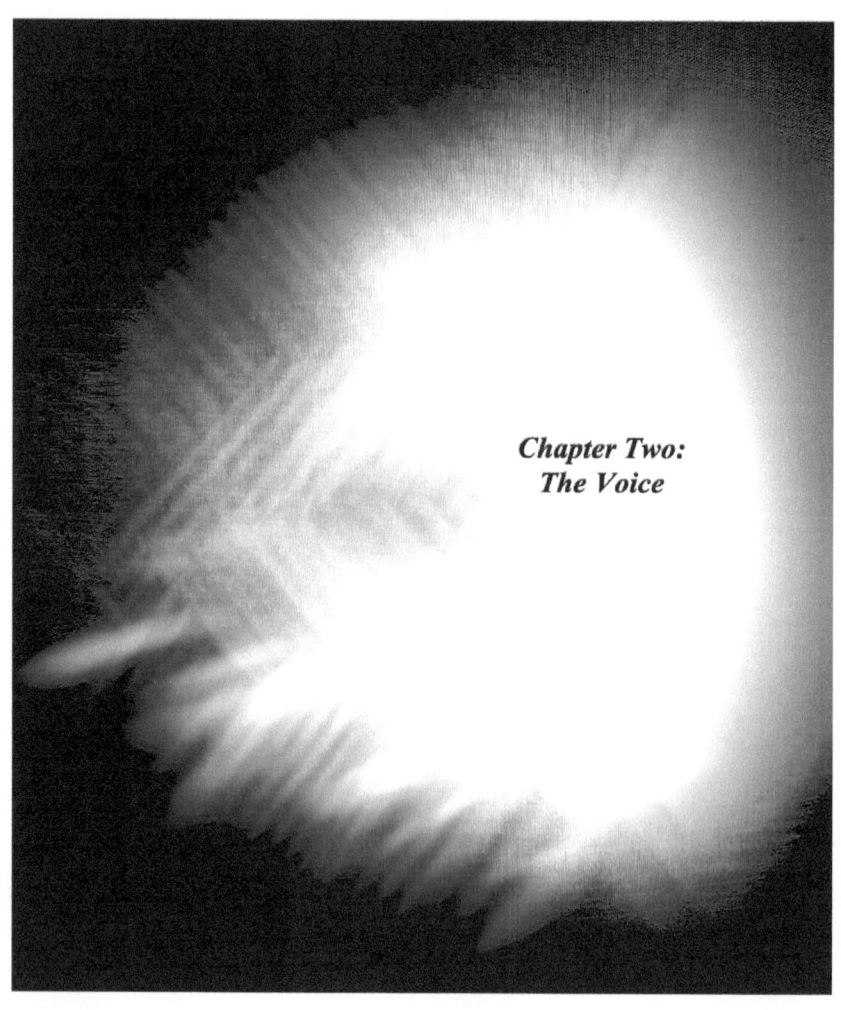

*Chapter Two:
The Voice*

XVI

Above the Water

Do you think that I'll let you drown me?
Do you think that I'll take your blows?
Don't you dare underestimate me,
I will not sink deep down below.
You better back up,
you better stay away,
I have had enough,
and this all ends today.
Erase our past,
all of our fights,
I am free at last,
and I will not die.
I have conquered your storm,
I have escaped your waves,
I am now reborn,
and I rise from the grave.

XVII

Barricade

Close all the doors,
barricade all the windows,
don't want anymore,
I want to escape the shadows.
Close all the blinds,
fortify my open heart.
I must be out of sight
before the storm starts.
My mind needs to breathe,
my mind needs relief.
I've sealed myself inside,
I just really want to hide.
Turn off all the lights,
I ignore the messages.
I won't be in the spotlight,
I have to clear my head.
Everyone can be so loud,

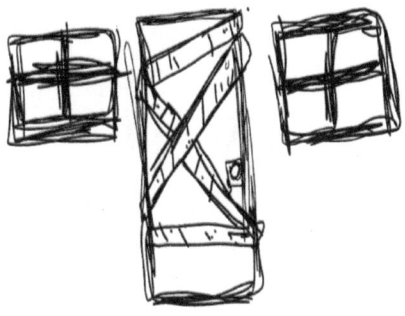

and they can be so noisy.
I shut the world out,
and now I can start the healing.

XVIII

A New Version

I look into my mirror, confident,
and I can see my reflection.
There used to be terror, panic,
but now there is a connection.
The person I was before was afraid,
but now is nothing but a shadow.
I give myself applause, praise,
and I overcame the sorrow.
I have a second chance,
a gift to start all over.
I found a rhythm, can dance,
and a new outlook on life forever.

XIX

Quiet

Quiet, let me sit in silence.
Quiet, I want to rejuvenate.
Quiet, let me hear the wind.
Quiet, the rain I appreciate.
Quiet, I hear birds singing.
Quiet, it is so nice, so lovely.
Quiet, I want to hear everything.
Quiet, I am connected, I'm happy.

XX

Subtract and Add

I get tired of hearing people complain.
If your life is so bad, do something about it.
Why do I even have to write this or even explain it?
It is okay to take a breath, chill, and sit.
Subtract all of the bad and all of the pain,
Add all of the great and make them fit.

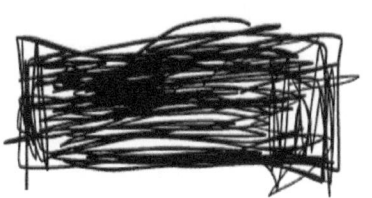

XXI

Crown

I found the strength to break out,
shatter the walls that hold me.
I am a warrior, a survivor,
so much stronger than I used to be.
I found the cure to my sickness,
I remedied all of the doubt.
I am a lion, a king,
and a crown I will wear, no doubt.

XXII

Who Are You?

You make me feel worthless,
pathetic, and the opposite of happy.
You can turn my day cloudy
and dark gray, making my mood crappy.
You know, I have always learned to forgive,
to love, and to try to move on and fly.
You know, you have me constantly questioning,
wondering, did I waste all of my time?
You know, I hope one day you empathize,
relate, and understand me better.
You know, I am fragile, I'm insecure,
and it's hard to keep it all together
You know, I try to see past all of the pain,
hate, and all of your mean conversations.
You know, you are the cause of my tears,
and silence, and you add more to my complications.

XXIII

Let You Go

so self-centered,
so unaware,
so arrogant,
and so unfair.
so predictable,
so selfish,
so terrible,
and so hellish.
so I let you go,
so I set you free,
so now you know,
so let me be.

XXIV

Wasteland

      Conversations used to be unique,
but you are too busy on your phone.
      Driving with the radio on was fun,
until you stopped singing with me.
      We were a green, lush, and glorious field,
but now we are a wasteland.
      Time to plant some new seeds,
      my life will be green without you.

XXV

Bleeding

I said I would die for you,
but I didn't mean it.
My heart and soul you use,
and you use them maliciously.
I said I would kill for you,
but you're the one killing me.
I am bleeding and bruised,
and you're draining all my energy.

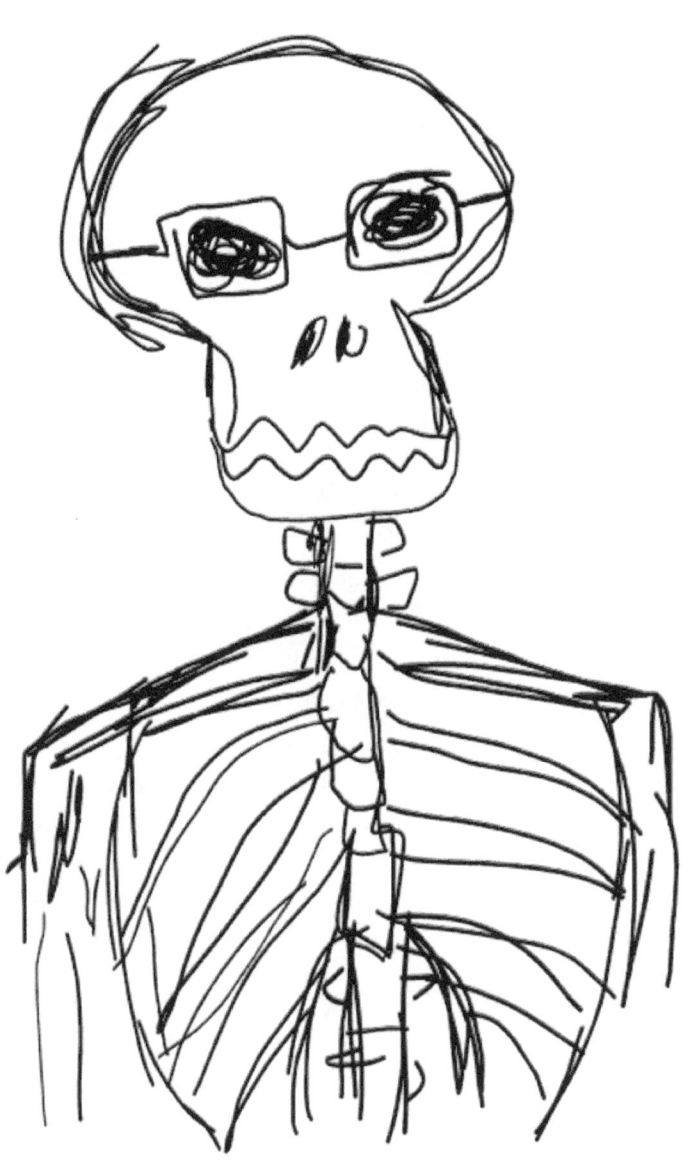

XXVI

I Won't Follow

I keep a safe distance from people,
not because I am afraid of them,
I just know how quickly they can change.
They are sweet like an angel,
then they turn evil, like the devil.
I've been this way my whole life,
call it a superpower I have,
I just know how people operate now.
People will manipulate me to get their way,
and that is a game I refuse to play.

XXVII

Recharge

I ran away from the city.
There are too many people, toxic, and so hard to breathe.
I need some uplifting.
There's so much chaos and hate surrounding me.
I have fled far into the woods,
a perfect getaway, escape. I needed this.
I can finally clear my head,
have peace of mind, all is calm, and I have found bliss.

XXVIII

Transcend

Daggers fall from the sky,
making their way to me,
I'm the target, and I can't hide.
They dig into my body,
I scream uncontrollably,
and I'm on the ground bloody.
They are my sins,
I regret my mistakes,
and the suffering begins.
Death will not be the end,
I pull the daggers out,
and I will heal and transcend.

XXIX

No Denying It

Your choice was final,
you decided the verdict,
you just became a rival,
and you want the world imperfect.
You want it to be like the 1950s,
you are in the past,
you are nothing but guilty,
and you are no different than the last.

XXX

A Sign

The fog surrounds me, taking me piece by piece,
it is slowly erasing all of me.
I try to fight it, but I am struggling,
does anyone see that this is troubling?
I can see no way out, and there is no escape,
the fog lets me go, and it's taking shape.
It manifests in front of my eyes,
it stares deep into my soul, and I can't hide.
Its eyes are red and filled with so much hate,
I freeze with fear. Is this my fate?
The entity starts to move closer,
I have a feeling that my life is over.
Its cold hands are around my neck, and I can't run,
I am suffocating; why am I the one?
Fire engulfs me, and I feel the scorching heat.
Is this the end? I've accepted defeat.
I woke up in a sweat, and it was a nightmare,

today I'll change and be thankful, I swear.

The Light

Chapter Three:
The Light

XXXI

Trust the Process

Life has been testing me so much lately,
I want to scream and throw things.
It would be ideal and satisfying,
but it would only be a relief for a moment.
I don't want to remain in this mindset,
and it is time to steer my mind in a new direction.
I will just have to trust the process
and continue down the path of success.

XXXII

Love

Love is a complicated entity,
it is suitable for others,
and to others, it is evil.
I've got to experience both sides of it.
Love is a complicated entity,
it causes extreme passion,
and it also causes extreme torture.
I got to witness both sides of it.
Love is a complex entity,
it is a safe place, a shelter,
and it can be a hurricane.
I've got to live on both sides of it.
Love is a complicated entity.

XXXIII

Ascension

There is a gust of wind,
with a scent of something sweet,
that blows my way, my direction.
I glance over at you,
you are taking pictures,
you are simply amazed by the ocean.
The sun shines down on me,
tanning my light brown body,
I am in the mood for some communication.
I smile and wave at you,
with some nervousness,
you smile and wave back without hesitation.
You head over to me,
with so much confidence,
you seem to have some good intentions.
You ask if you may sit,
I smile and nod,

you sit next to me, and there's no tension.
We exchange our names,
we talk for hours,
and from there, we started our ascension.

XXXIV

Inner Strength

Reason,
this anger will pass,
you feel it internally,
but it will not last.
Think positive,
and this self-doubt isn't genuine.
You feel negative,
but that isn't you.
You are stronger,
more robust than you know,
you already know this,
show your strength and grow.

XXXV

Realization

Do you ever want to disappear?
Run far away and start all over?
As the years continue forward,
the idea is becoming more apparent.
I thought that I'd found my place,
I thought that I'd establish my peace,
but there is so much more to do, to see,
and there is a lot more to this life.
I want to experience a new beginning,
to be able to do the things I want.
I want to live my life without guilt,
and I will chase the life I've always wanted.

XXXVI

Truth and Forgiveness

The truth is such a potent weapon,
I have done some terrible things
and I have admitted to all of them.
I spoke my truth and wished for forgiveness,
and I know that it was from my heart.
They say, *"thank you, and all is fine."*

Now I await their truth and their apologies.
The truth will eventually come to the surface,
and when it does, I will say, *"thank you, and all is fine."*

XXXVII

Rainstorms

Hello, again, gray clouds,
It's always lovely to see you again.
I am lying on the ground,
all my scars you mend.
Your tears begin to fall,
they land gently on my face,
I don't mind them at all,
I want to stay in this place.
You light up all of the skies,
and it's always a breathtaking show.
You shout sometimes,
and you make everyone know.
I feel comfort when you're here,
I don't have the will to flee,
I am safe, and I have no fear,
this place is where I want to be.

XXXVIII

Beacon of Hope

There is darkness in the world,
people have evil intentions,
people can't open up their hearts,
and it has my full attention.
There is fear inside my heart,
people need to be less self-centered,
people must open up their minds,
and all the hate must surrender.
There is still time to be a light,
a light that heals the globe,
a light that shines and never fades,
be a light and a beacon of hope.

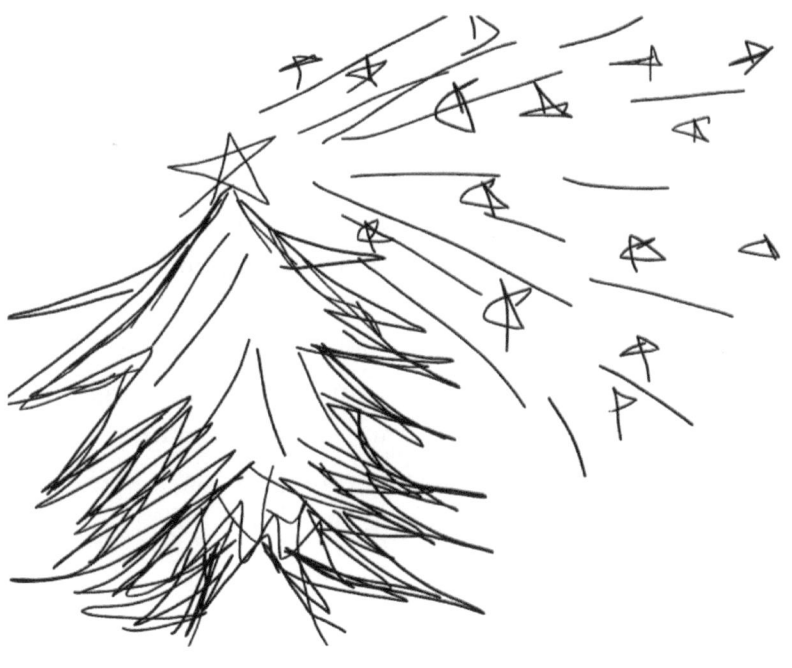

XXXIX

Growing Up

Usually, I am one to take a beating,
but now that I am older, it's crippling.
It's harder to take the pain and run,
now I get hurt and get stunned.
It's apparent that I am more sensitive,
I am less combative and less argumentative.
When things go wrong, go astray,
I hope for nothing but a better day.

XL

Fireworks

We don't wait to combust,
and we've never been the same.
We always want some lust,
so bright and just like a flame.
Our flame is so strong,
we are full of heat.
This place is where we belong,
and there's no need to retreat.
You have a loud soul,
I have a quiet heart.
We have the same goals,
and we keep creating art.
Our love is intense,
from mild to berserk.
Let the show commence,
and we are just like fireworks.

XLI

The Better Part of Me

When I'm feeling low,
you make me feel so high.
When I cannot breathe,
you fill my lungs with air.
When I lose my cool,
you chill me out somehow.
When I cannot laugh,
you bust out all your jokes.
When I've given up,
you pick me up again.
When I cannot love,
you love me till I do.

XLII

Undying Love

Within my body,
there lies my heart.
Within my heart,
there lies undying love.
Within undying love,
there is only you.

Within only you,
there is only me.

XLIII

Keep Them Forever

Life is very unfair,
and it doesn't care who you are.
Every day is a gift,
and treasure life like it's art.
Hold every ounce of it,
and hold it very tight.
Make sure to cherish it
because it can disappear overnight.
Take a photograph,
and remember those moments.
Keep them close to your heart,
and save all those components.
Love those memories,
and don't let them drift apart.
Keep them forever
because they were exceptional from the start.

XLIV

Talk to Me

Talk to me,
tell me your problems,
tell me your goals.
Open up to me,
speak your truth,
and say what's on your mind.
I'm a safe space,
I'll be a safety net,
I'll be nothing but a friend.
Express yourself,
show me your art,
show me your ambitions.

XLV

Some Inspiration

It doesn't stay cloudy forever,
a light will shine through.
Things will come together,
you will become brand new.
The storm will subside,
and the sun will show itself.
Things will be alright.
Just smile and be your best self.

XLVI

A Light in the Darkness

Suffocating darkness surrounds you,
and a chilling breeze goes up your spine.
You thought you'd escaped its cold embrace,
but it finds you again and won't unwind.
"Someone, anyone, please help me!"
You scream as if you can't find a way out.
A wave of terror engulfs you,
you thought this was your end.
"I'm here! Follow my voice!"
I scream as my voice fills your ears.
You see a slight glint of light. You fight,
and my voice fills you with hope.
I continue screaming for you.
My voice fuels the fire inside of you.
You pull away from the darkness,
you start sprinting towards the light.
Without looking back, you smile.

My voice is louder, and the light grows brighter.
With one final push, you reach for my hand,
I grab your hand, and then darkness vanishes.

Skye is Filipino-American, a member of the LGBTQ+ community, and a person who struggles with mental illness. Get a glimpse inside the mind of a person who knows how it is to feel alone, different, and unheard. Skye hopes this piece of work will be the beacon of light for those who are lost, afraid, and feeling hopeless.

www.ingramcontent.com/pod-product-compliance
Lightning Source LLC
Chambersburg PA
CBHW020337010526
44119CB00001B/12